Webcam Models Make Alot of Money!

 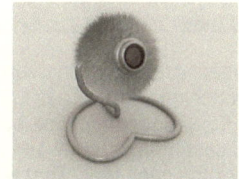

Online Employer: Hiring for online models!
<u>**Salary Potential: $60.00-$120.00 an hr.**</u>

Be youou can choose your hours and work from home!
All you need is a computer, a webcam and an Internet
connection and you could start earning today!

We offer one of the best platforms for online web cam
models to make money.
NO GIMMICK OR MLM!

Written By: Kiesha Richcreek

When you read this book and use everything listed this book
should help your income!

Yes, you can make some SERIOUS cash with webcam modeling

Webcam modeling is the online version of video porno, except for the fact that people are watching what you do LIVE. The typical webcam performer will dress herself up in sexy clothing, put on some pretty makeup, sit down and talk with a few potential customers, then when she is taken into private, she will perform sexual acts for the customer. That is where the term webcam actress comes from. During private chat, the performer will do as the customer requests and be paid for her acting. Keep in mind that males can also be webcam models too, but females are definitely the majority of the sexes.

A good webcam or camcorder is an absolute necessity. You can start with a lower end model, but upgrade as soon as possible. At least one lamp with an adjustable neck is needed to light yourself correctly. Adult webcam viewers will not become regulars if your image is grainy and dark. You will need a high speed internet connection, Comcast, AT&T DSL is okay but you want a quality show and a place in your home where you can have relax and have privacy. Try to start with at least three pieces of lingerie and three nice but not too revealing outfits. You will need to register with the major instant messengers - Yahoo, AIM, MSN, etc.
Chatrooms used to be a great places to find webcam shows and sell shows independently. In the last few years they've become overrun with bots and women selling shows for other models on commission. This makes it very hard to sell 1 on 1, but it is a good idea to stake out a few adult chat

rooms in your niche. Stream your cam but don't show any flesh - not even breasts! Be careful of time wasters, and skeptical of men who will only buy a show after a "preview". Often, this is only to scam a free cam show.
Craigslist

Craigslist and other free classified ad sites with erotic sections are excellent resources. Bookmark several cities and post each day, at least once a day. Graphical ads, those saved as a JPEG, work better for posting ads faster.

Camgirlshide is a site that lists independent cam girls. You can list for free, but you will be reviewed to check for authenticity. Once you have your chat profiles ready, (Yahoo, AIM, etc.) go here to register your information on, as well as to learn more about selling cam shows independently.

Paypal will suspend your account for sales of anything adult related, so to accept payment instantly you'll have to look for a paypal alternative. Ikobo and E-pasporte are two that are widely used. You can also accept gift certificates as forms of payment, but you will need to list them on your taxes as well.

Hundreds of webcam sites, or adult webcam hosts, exist to choose from. The payment methods and rates vary, but most take a comission of 30 - 50% of your sales. Others will pay you a flat rate for each show. Two of the largest (and busiest) are Niteflirt and IMLive.

IMLive is always hiring for webcam operators. However, to say that you work "for" the site somewhat inaccurate. Sites like IMlive.com host thousands of profiles and provide the software and billing system. You sign up, create your profile, and set your per minute rate. IMLive takes roughly 50% of your per minute rate. You can increase your take by bringing in your own customers.

Listings on Niteflirt involve a phone based system. Niteflirt.com began as a phone sex portal, and independent phone sex operators began offering webcam features as they became more popular. You will have to use your own software, such as Yahoo Messenger or Eyeball Chat, to stream a cam to your caller. Niteflirt has a merit system as well as a bidding system for placement in their listings. Your "bid per click" will be billed to your Niteflirt account, and the higher ranking you desire for your profile the more you'll pay for each click through.

Once you have the basic equipment, you have to decide if you will work for a webcam host site, or sell webcam shows independently. It is possible to do both once you get some experience. It is faster to get started independently, but your traffic and results might be more predictable on a host site.

Expect downtimes on any adult webcam host.. Most performers offset this by streaming their cam feed to more than one site, which is also a good strategy to use when working indpendently. Your webcam's software probably doesn't come with this ability, but a freeware program called Splitcam

makes it possible. Splitcam is available from many reputable freeware sites, such as CNET's Download.com.

Never use your real name, city, or any identifying information with a customer. You should have a separate persona complete with history and likes/dislikes if the viewer wants to get to know you. Never agree to meet a viewer or give out your home phone or cell number. AIM and Yahoo allow PC to phone calling for a small fee and PC to PC calling for free. Never use email addresses that you have used in your personal life. Check with legal requirements to ensure that you are keeping adequate records.

Letting your exhibitionist side out to play can be profitable and fun. If you remember to treat giving webcam shows as a business, while still being personable and giving excellent customer service, you will build a steady clientele

No revenue split with a host site.
Faster payment (many host sites only pay once a minimum has been reached)
More control over what you can say/do in your show

More legal liability
Must spend more time negotiating payment with customers
Customers are more likely to try to haggle
More time spent marketing your profiles initially.

There are many advantages to becoming a webcam model. You get to set your own hours, work from the comfort and privacy of your home, show off your sexy self, and make more money than you ever thought possible! Being a webcam model will not only free you from financial woes, but it will boost your self-confidence through the roof! You will be complimented and basically worshiped by all of your customers. It makes for a great job.

To be eligible to be a webcam model, you must be at least 18 years of age or older, have a high-speed Internet connection, own or have access to a good quality web camera, and be open-minded. Webcam models must be open-minded because you will be faced with all types of people with all types of fetishes/sexual fantasies. You must know how to "work it" and keep the customer coming back. If you cannot handle people talking dirty to you or making rude comments at times, you will not make it as a webcam model.

Webcam models make tons of cash, no joke! If you are willing to do this job it will pay you 10 times more than any other online job would. Not only can you make multiple dollars a minute, but some sites even have a tip system where the customer can tip you along with paying for private sessions! That way you will earn more cash and get to your minimum payout faster.

Speaking of minimum payouts, both studios and cam sites have them. You must make a certain amount of money to be able to request your money, but there are a few sites that have their minimum set very low. So really, this is your best bet if you are in need of emergency cash and are willing to show some skin to pay your bills. The average cam model makes anywhere from $40-$120 an hour!

I will start off by explaining what a studio for webcam models is. No, it is not an actual place where you go in and work. Some people may do that, but most will not. A studio basically gets paid to promote you and recruit new models. Any new model that is registered on a site through a studio will earn that studio some major cash. Studios will receive a percentage of the earnings the model makes while webcam modeling. It is not a bad thing to work through a studio because some will promote you for free (which means more cash), but they do get to take a cut out of your earnings and control how much money you end up with. Some studios will rip you off and some will be generous.

Why you should work directly with a site instead of a studio (this is only my opinion).
After experiencing some bad studios that always lagged on paying and cut way to much pay, I decided to give direct modeling a go. I found a few sites, experimented with them, and finally found the one I wanted to stick with. Overall, it has been a great experience and I am making a lot more money than I was at first (by the way, there are links to reliable cam sites at the end of this article). If at all possible, stick to direct modeling for a site unless you feel that a studio is the right choice for you.

Here is where it gets somewhat hard. After thoroughly reading all of the above, you might have a slight idea of what you want to do. It's OK if you don't. Take some time and figure out what will personally work best for you.

If you have chosen to work through a studio, I suggest you check out Jasmin Studios.

They have a high 60% payout and always pay on time. They were the last studio I worked with and I received nothing but good support from them.

BECOME AN EXOTIC DANCER TO MAKE YOUR MOVES SHINE

Tools of the trade
Other than your body, which we'll get into later, the tools of the trade are clothing, makeup, and shoes. In dancing, as with any other trade, it never pays to buy cheap tools-they don't work well, they break and you'll just have to replace them anyway.

Heels are your first purchase. Minimum height is 3 inches- anything shorter and your gut will stick out and your legs will look like tree trunks. Look for a shoe with a plastic one-piece sole and heel. Shoes with the leather and wood heels are much more elegant but after the second night of dancing on them the heels tend to flex too much and put a lot of stress on your knees and back. Open toes tend to be more comfortable but if you're going to wear them you have to make sure your toenails are painted and trimmed. Putting no-slip rubber pads on the bottom of the shoe is a good idea- it prevents embarrassing falls on slippery stages.

Bottoms come in a few different varieties: choose according to your tastes, club rules, etc. Almost all clubs require thongs. A dancing bottom can be purchased through mail order (see Note 1) or at stores that carry them. Girls who try dancing in underwear or a swimsuit bottom always look tacky. Buy the right kind. Some topless clubs have rules against g-strings (string sides and back) because they tend to not provide enough coverage to comply with local laws.

Some clubs don't care what kind of dress you wear- lots of girls wear neon spandex micro minis etc. Other clubs called "gown clubs" have more strict rules and generally require these sort of slutty evening gowns. These gowns like the bottoms need to be custom made or ordered- nothing from the department store will cut it. One thing that I cannot emphasis enough- NEVER ever wear an asymmetrical dress (hem cut at an angle or one shoulder strap). As most people know, men subconsciously look at certain physical attributes as signs of good genetics and a desirable partner -- boobs, hips etc. They also look for something anthropologists call "Bilateral Symmetry" which means that your arms and legs are the same length, your torso is straight etc. An asymmetrical dress throws this off. It may look nice but you can actually chart the drop in earnings on a night to night basis.

Hair. Neck down it's all gotta go. Leave a little patch on top. Even if you're only dancing topless you have to keep it pretty clear. It looks really gross when little strands of hair stick out from the side of your G-string. Most girls wax but if it's a real problem some girls get electrolysis (ouch either way). I had mine done with a laser with good results. I know a lot of other girls are doing the same these days. Stubble is a definite no-no and shaving several days a week causes irritation and ingrown hair. So I'd stick with wax, laser or electrolysis.

Make up is pretty easy- most girls already know how to do that. Some clubs have their own makeup artists- they generally do a good job but tend to make all the girls look the same. A vital tool of the trade is body makeup. This is used to cover any blemishes that you might have on your body. If your club does a lot of pole or floor work you will need body makeup- This kind of dancing causes a lot of leg bruising.

Your body
What kind of shape you're in makes a bigger difference in your earnings than anything else. An hour of exercise a day can mean $200 more a night. It's important that you understand that your body is how you earn a living, as such you have to take very good care of it. In the world of strip clubs the name of the game is low bodyfat. Sure some men like extra padding but no one likes cheese. It's an unfortunate truth but the slimmer you are the more money you will make. You don't have to be fashion model skinny but you do have to be tight if you expect to make good money. I personally find that a combination of yoga and weight training is ideal for the kind of look that men like.

I do Ashtanga yoga four days a week, run one-day and weight training one day. The most effective weight training exercises for woman are squats, lunges and stiff-leg or sumo deadlifts. None of these lifts should be done on machines- free weights only. Machines are no where near as effective. Train heavy and train hard. Yoga and dancing are both very catabolic activities (they break down muscle tissue) you will not get bulky.

I use the following:
Squats 3 sets of 20 reps, 120 seconds rest between sets.
Stiff-leg deadlifts 3 sets of 10 reps, 120 seconds rest between sets.
Rest 5 minutes
Dumbbell lunges 4 sets of 12 reps, 90 seconds rest between sets
Hanging crunches 4 sets 90 seconds rest between sets

The squats should be to failure, it should be VERY hard to hit 20. Like having a baby hard. Squats will make a bigger change in your physique then anything else. When you do your yoga and running do it in the morning on an empty stomach. If you have a real fat problem an hour of running or jump rope a day before breakfast with a low/no carb diet can take of a lot of fat in a short period of time.

One of the problems with maintaining relatively low levels of body fat is that there is no way to have "spot" fat loss. It's all or nothing. As you lose the fat off your butt and thighs you also lose your breasts- often as much as a cup size. This is the reason that many dancers choose to have breast augmentation. Unfortunately some people like to tut-tut and shake their heads at women who get implants and imply all sorts of nasty things about the morals of women who would actually care about the way they look. Implants should be a choice based on how you feel- not how other people feel about you having them. There are lots of men who rail against implants, about how they don't like them and how they can always tell the difference, but that's bullshit. The only time they can tell is if it's a bad implant job, since they think the good jobs are real they assume that all implants look bad. Most men will tell you they don't like implants but in my experience in real life they like them a great deal. The girls I work with estimate it was an additional 20% in earnings after they got their augmentation and that most men seem to find them much, much, more attractive. Of course you shouldn't just get implants just to make more money, you should get them so you feel good about yourself. Some people may say that's a bad way to feel good about yourself but you could be doing a whole lot worse and more harmful things. Is it "fair"? No, of course not, life's not fair. It's also not "fair" that women prefer muscular men to fat ones. In an ideal world we wouldn't care about that but the reality is that our society places a great deal of value in physical attractiveness. Having large breasts makes you feel sexy, attractive and desirable. If men could have an operation to do the same there would be a line going around the block and Medicaid would cover it.

Different diets work for different people. Regardless of what you choose it has to be something you can stay on permanently. You can't just diet when you think your getting fat, as a dancer you have to maintain a consistantly low level of bodyfat. For me carbs are the problem. The only real carb heavy meal I eat is breakfast, I usually have a bowl of cereal or hot oatmeal. Then with lunch slightly less, usually just a sandwich with some whole wheat bread. For dinner almost none, a very small scoop of rice or vegetables with a small steak or chicken breast. I avoid salad, pasta and other high-carb meals. I occasionally eat fried chicken or hamburgers, I just keep the portions very small and try to eat it early in the day. Avoid low-fat foods or at least read the labels carefully, they tend to have a lot of sugar and nothing gets you fat faster than sugar- not even fat. I also try and break my meals down into several small ones. If it's a sandwich or something I eat one half then and one half an hour or two later- this helps you metabolize your food better. This may not work for you but I know many dancers on this or very similar programs who are able to stay in very good shape even with lousy genetics (I was 20lbs heavier before I started doing this and I've been able to maintain my weight for several years). The point is you need to find something that does work, staying in good shape is critical to your livelihood.

Auditioning and dancing

Your first and most important concern is to find a suitable club. It needs to be a place where you feel safe and comfortable. It doesn't matter how good the money is, if the place makes you feel bad about yourself you'll be miserable working there. Go to the Ultimate Strip Club List and look for clubs in your area. The reviews will give you a very good idea of whether it's a place you want to work. i.e. If the guy says, "Wow, it was great. This girl let me feel her up" It's obviously not a place you want to work. Looking for a good club is like looking for any other job- you want to get the most money for the least amount of work.

So what kind of money will you be making? If you're dancing for shift pay in a blue collar "titty bar" you'll make about $150 a night. A go-go or "cage" dancer at a regular nightclub might make $200 a night but she'll be dancing almost all night. Some girls might prefer that- you don't have to work for tips or talk to the guys. A girl dancing for tips and drink commission in a nude club makes between $200 to $600. A pretty, well-spoken girl who knows the business will make between $400 to $800 at a topless "gown" club. (Gown club refers to a club like TENS were the girls wear gowns and the clientele is more upscale). A feature dancer whose done some magazine and movie work might make $1500 a night. These numbers are just a rough guide. They're based on my own experience dancing in New York- earnings vary a lot from state to state. It also depends on the club, your verbal skills and your looks- in that order. Believe it or not the girls who make the most money stripping are rarely the prettiest. It's the ones who know how to tell the guys what they want to hear who make the real money. All without ever having to actually do anything.

There's no way around it, the first time you get on stage you're going to be scared out of your wits. DON'T have a drink to "calm your nerves". It is very habit forming- I've worked with girls who can't start the night without a few shots of "liquid courage". Drinking on the job is a really bad idea; it can let you permit guys to take liberties you would not otherwise allow - including getting in their car after work. If a guy offers to buy you a drink ask for a Diet Coke or juice. If the management complains say you're Mormon or something. I'm not trying to be condescending or imply you can't drink responsibly, it's just that I've seen some bad stuff.

When you're ready, just show up at the club and say you'd like an audition, be nice to whoever is working the door- they frequently screen girls for the managers. They may ask you to come back on another night but they normally just put you on one of the side stages. One of the managers will watch you dance for a few songs then talk to you a little bit to make sure you've got a good attitude, etc.

As far as dancing is concerned a lot depends on the club. You have to see the way the other strippers dance. Some clubs don't allow floor or pole work, while in others they do all that plus shower and lesbian shows. Even if you're straight, the lesbian shows can be a lot of fun but they are never mandatory. Most clubs work on a standard 3 song set. That means for the first song when you're on stage you have all your clothes on, the second, you remove something and for the last you wear either nothing or just a thong depending on whether it's a nude or topless club. There is not a whole lot to dancing- at least the basics. You do not need lessons or to buy a video. Just watch what the other girls are doing, you'll pick it up in a few minutes. Just avoid anything showy or dramatic until you know how to do it right. Before you audition I would suggest trying out some of your moves in front of a mirror then getting some constructive criticism from a guy (they can be very helpful and are usually delighted to assist). Once you get to know the other dancers they will generally help out and show you some of the trickier moves. In my opinion it can be fun perfecting your dancing technique but not something you should spend a lot of time at. Guys appreciate a good dancer but seldom buy dances from a girl based on her dancing ability. You're better off spending the time working out and improving your physique.

Making money
At most clubs you walk around and ask the customers if they'd like a private dance (or lap dance depending on the club). Some clubs just have stage dancing. Often there is a private area that you can go for a dance. Be careful, though, the dim lights and the privacy tend to make the guys a little frisky. Not in a bad or scary way just in a way that may need to be corrected. The most important thing to do when you're dancing is to SMILE AND MAKE EYE CONTACT. Nothing turns a guy off faster then a dancer strolling bored around the stage while staring vacantly off into space. Try to make each guy you're dancing for think he's the ONLY guy you're dancing for. This is how the pros make the big bucks.

At many clubs a significant part of your nightly earnings comes from dances. Most of the time the customer will pay for you to sit and talk with them as well. Guys vary a lot but it's always important to be attentive. Nobody likes to feel like they're being ignored. Most guys are pretty nice and easy to talk to. Provided you're a good listener and act interested, it's no problem. Then you get the guys who aren't trying to be obnoxious- they just don't have the best social skills. They will sit and alternate between nagging you to go out with them and lying about how much money they have, how many places they've traveled, how important they are in their company, etc. Simpering and looks of wide-eyed wonder come in handy at this point. Some guys are an absolute pleasure to sit with: they buy dances, they visit on a regular basis, and best of all they're lots of fun to talk too. It's guys like this who really make it all worth while.

When dancing it's important to stay motivated, at most clubs you are an independent contractor. You won't get fired if you don't work hard and no one will say anything if you decide to hang out at the bar and talk all night. You need to treat it like a job- not a social experience. Decide on what time and how long you will have dinner for, the rest of the time work the floor as hard as you can. Make sure you always get at least 8 hours of sleep so you're not tired. You'll look and feel better. Set a clear goal, try to get 4 dances and hour, as you get better set higher goals for yourself. Never assume a passive approach and wait for them to call you over, stay moving and keep working. If it's hard and you just can't get motivated make a game of it, make bets with other girls on who can get the most dances. Promise yourself ice cream if you reach a certain mark, whatever you have to do to stay motivated and keep earning money.

Learning how to properly break the ice and get invited to sit with a customer takes time. Most girls tend to just walk around to every guy in the room and ask "Wanna dance?" and then when he says no walk off. This is the exact wrong approach. Every guy in that room has enough money for at least one dance- you just have to find the right words to get them to buy one. "Wanna dance?" can work in a very crowded room or if a guy is already interested but it will do absolutely nothing to convince a guy who was uninterested to change his mind. It's too easy to say no to. To start with, choose your targets, who is looking at you the most when you are on stage or dancing for other customers? Talk to the bartender and the floor hosts: who has an open tab or has been spending a lot of money? If a bartender or floor hosts gives you a good lead and you make money ALWAYS tip them at the end of the night- that way next time they will go to you first when they see a big spender. When you approach your prospective customer try and say anything but "Wanna dance?": would you like some company?, would you like if I joined you? If the room is slow and he seems reluctant put a very slight push on. If he says he's not interested ask if he would mind if you just sat down and rested your feet for a minute- you're "not used to these heels". Few men are going to say no to that, and the "not used to these heels" implies that you're a new dancer and invites conversation. If 10 minutes go by and he still doesn't buy a dance don't ask- just say "I'm sorry, I've got to get back to work- it's been nice talking to you okay?" This implies that you didn't consider sitting with him work, a slight bit of flattery that will probably get you a dance later. Think of this approach as "seeding"in that you may not get the dance then, but chances are you will later. After a half-hour of "wanna dance" from the other girls he's going to wish for your company again and probably be willing to pay for it. Or even the next time he comes in yours will be the familiar face. With this approach it's important you not spend too long with them- keep them hungry. Unless they're paying don't sit with them longer then 10 to 15 minutes and only that long if the room is very slow. If they're used to getting it for free it's going to be hard to get them to pay for it. You're friendly and available- they just have to be willing to pay for it.

Never ever, sit on your own or hang out at the bar talking to other dancers. At any given time you should be either sitting with a customer, moving to another customer or on stage. If you're just standing around they will assume you're not busy and it will be VERY hard to get a customer to pay for your time because "you're not doing anything anyway". Look busy, if they think other men want you then they will want you.

It's important you have respect for the money they give you, so much money changes hands that girls often forget what it represents. Let's say your customer earns $40,000 a year after taxes- probably about average income for a stripclub patron in NYC. That works out to around $20 an hour. If a customer sits with you and you make $100, that's 5 hours of his time. If a handyman came to your house and fixed thing for 5 hours you'd say "thank you" right? Always thank the customer and make sure he knows you mean it. Even if $100 doesn't seem like a lot of money to you to the average customer it is.

One last thing, don't screw with guys' heads. It's not cool, you can make money without doing it. I see lots of girls who string guys along implying they'll go out with them if they just visit a few more times or laying on sob stories about their sick children or parents. Don't do it, there is never any reason for you to lie as a dancer. After a few repetitions it gets very fake and you just come off as a greedy gold digger. If you want customers to treat you with respect you should treat them with respect. If they are disrespectful just walk away, there is no reason for you to sink to their level. There are more then enough good men who will to pay you to sit, talk and laugh with them and when you dance they will treat you like a goddess. As customers they deserve your courtesy and if they don't respect you in return they don't deserve to have you spend time with them.

Safety

Safety is a critical issue for dancers. Many men do not understand that what we sell is a fantasy or feel that our employment makes us fair game for unwanted attentions. The six dumbest words that can leave a woman's mouth are "I can take care of myself". No you can't, and get any notion that you're some kind of tough girl out of your head. Men are bigger, stronger and meaner. They've been beating and raping women for thousands of years now and have pretty much got it down pat. Your little kickboxing lessons at the health club will not help you. If a grown man hits you full force you will be knocked unconscious and very likely break the bones in your face. Do not ever make safety decisions based on your opinion of your ability to defend yourself.

I personally think that carrying weapons or taking martial art, self-defense classes etc. are a bad idea for most women. The most effective way to survive is to be scared; anything that makes you brave makes you more likely to walk into a dangerous situation. If you have a gun in your purse you might be more likely to take that shortcut home, or take a ride with a man you don't know very well or any number of risky things. If you're scared you're careful, if you're careful you don't get into trouble. If you are a feature dancer, have a very public presence (website or modeling), or have had problems with a stalker a gun may be something you want to consider purchasing. You need to be trained in it's use and practice with it at a firing range at least once every few months. Don't bother carrying one unless you comfortable with the idea of killing someone. That's what guns are for, you're not going to be shooting knives out of anyone's hands, you're going to be trying to make a hole in the center of their torso. If you have small hands like me you can have a gunsmith machine a trigger guard that will comfortable fit your finger but too small for the finger of a grown man. But I would like to emphasize, most women are far better off not carrying a gun. Only if you are in a position of constantly being exposed to unavoidable danger is it an option.

One never wishes to blame the victim but every single girl I know without exception who has ever gotten into trouble was doing something most women would consider risky or just plain stupid. Don't take chances- the stakes are too high.

As a dancer leaving the club after work is the time when you are most vulnerable. I have only gotten scared twice at work. On both occasions it was when an overly enthusiastic customer decided to wait for me outside the club after closing. On both occasions the men were just confused about the nature of what a dancer does and were quickly dealt with by security. This being said transportation is a critical safety issue that you really have to think about. Going to work is not a problem- they can't really see where you are coming from. Leaving is when you have to be most vigilant. Public transportation is out of the question, it's too easy to be followed and is rarely safe at the hours you'll be riding. I'd suggest sharing a cab with one of the other girls. If you decide to drive, make very sure that your car is reliable, last thing you need is a break down on an empty road at 3AM. A cell phone is a good thing to have and if you just use it for emergencies it only costs about $15 a month. Make sure when you register you car you do it to another address (friend, parent, etc.). That way if some creep takes down your license plate number he can't find out your home address.

For obvious reasons never give any personal info to anyone who knows you as a dancer- including other dancers. There are dancers and bouncers who will give the information to customers for money or as a favor. There is no reason anyone needs to know anything but your stage name. Don't tell them where you live or what school you go to no matter how trust worthy they seem. Once that information is out it's very difficult to put back in the box.

List your business Websites: _____
_____
_____

YOU SHOULD TRY YOUR BEST TO LOOK ATTRACTIVE

Hi there, this is some VERY important info about Cybermate.

I do not know what experience you have with camming so I will send everything. Newbie's listen to the information given.

As I am aware Cybermate TV (CTV) has NOT been regularly paying its Chat Hosts since about March/April 2005. I know more than 30 Chat Hosts who have not been paid. They include new chat hosts and chat hosts that have worked there for more than a year. Some of their pay stopped in February 2005.

I further understand that non payment may go back as far as 2002.

It seems that CTV often will pay for the first 2 weeks, often at a reduced rate, but never pay again

Cumasutra had a message up saying she wasn't paid and was promised that they will pay her soon but she still hasn't been paid and I don't think that will happen. Cumasutra had a message up again yesterday saying she had not been paid.

Cumasutra message said "...Hello dear support Anne Romanov! Will pay to me please, I wait the third month. Answer my letter. I look forward ".

Others have had similar messages up including a studio.

36dd was telling guys in her chat that CTV did not pay.

Curvylady has said that the site does not pay chat hosts.

TrulyGirl also said that the site did not pay her.

Cralizek1 is telling all guys the site does not pay and to go to another site.

CTV was closed during mid 2005 for about 2 months because it was not paying chat hosts and studios.

Also please be very careful of these sites:

http://www.extasycams.com/ a friend said she did NOT get paid by this site.

http://www.tabulivecams.com whilst I cannot say the site does not pay two Chat Hosts have told me that they have had shows that have NOT shown on their earnings and one has said that she has NOT been paid. Also the site owner, Jason, has said in open chat that he watches and records all private shows. One Chat Host told me that he actually gave her directions when she was in a private show with a viewer.

These links may help you.

http://www.adult-webcam-faq.com/
If you want to read about Cybermate TV (CTV) in the forum, click on forum in the right corner. You will have to register, it is free, and then click search in the forum and search for Cybermate when the results come up scroll down the page Cybermate is listed 4 or 5 times. If you read, it gives you a good history about the bad ethics of the site.

http://www.adult-webcam-faq.com/
This one is the site that gives a list of sites and a review of each site. Click on Reviews at the top of the page.

Detail eBook on how a model makes money!

There are thousands of sites on the net. These are sites that I have been given by girls as reputable that pay.

http://www.streamray.com epassporte
http://www.cams4us.com
http://www.imlive.com epassporte
http://www.px24.co.uk
http://www.islive.com
http://www.crazywebcam.com
http://www.livecambuster.com
http://www.streamate.com epassporte
http://www.joyourself.com epassporte
http://www.livejasmin.com epassporte
http://www.webcams.com
http://www.adultwork.co.uk
http://www.camcontacts.com No Philippines or Romania
http://www.cozycontacts.com
http://www.niteflirt.com
http://websfinest.com
http://private.camz.com
http://www.clubxlive.com
http://adultcammodels.com
http://www.juicynetwork.com
 http://www.realgirlsoncam.com/
http://www.webcamlive.co.uk
http://www.camgirlshide.com
http://www.xxxcambabes.com
http://www.showsalon.com
http://www.sweetlovecams.com
http://www.camgirlsxposed.com
http://www.camsturbate.com

You should also consider doing shows in Yahoo or MSN and using iKobo or epassporte or Western Union for the payment method. You charge $1.49 in CTV and IF CTV pay you will get either 90cents or $1.00 depending on how you do your free chat. In Yahoo or MSN you could charge $1.25 and get $1.25. You get more money and the guy pays less. You both win. You can use CTV to get viewers to MSN/Yahoo, tell guys that you only do pvts there not on CTV.

(How to get paid) - Important

PayPal
http://www.paypal.com/
ePassporte

https://www.epassporte.com/
Western Union
http://www.westernunion.com

If you want to have some fun and possibly get some guys for pvt in Yahoo or
MSN have a look at this site   http://www.rude.com/   I am not convinced that
sites like this or Pal Talk   http://www.paltalk.com/   or the heaps of other similar
actually are worthwhile because guys there usually want it ALL for free, but for
fun maybe.

http://www.splitcamera.com
This site has software called SplitCam. It allows you to be on more than one site
at the same time with video on all with one cam. It also has a very good built in
pan and zoom feature. You use the mouse wheel, much better than others. It is
FREE.

http://manycam.com/index.php
This site has software called Manyam. It allows you to be on more than one site at the same time
with video on all with one cam. It has some effects you can add. To remove the"ManyCam.com"
logo go to Options, Effects, Text over video and uncheck the box.

http://www.broadcaster.com
This site has software called StudioPro. It allows you to be on more than one site at the same
time with video on all with one cam. It also has a movie maker and capture facility. (Download
under Tools)

You should also make sure you have good anti-virus and anti-spyware software.
There are FREE versions available which are very good and better than most of
the better-known brands.

You can download FREE anti-virus software from the following addresses:
http://www.free-av.com
(Antivirus® Personal Edition Classic it is the one I use)
http://free.grisoft.com/doc/1
(AVG)
http://www.comodogroup.com/products/free_products.html
(Comodo AntiVirus)

You can download FREE anti-spyware from the following addresses:
http://www.microsoft.com/athome/security/spyware/software/default.mspx
(Windows Defender Beta 2)
http://free.grisoft.com/doc/1
AVG Anti-spyware
http://www.safer-networking.org

(Spybot Search and Destroy)

You can download FREE anti-spam software from the following addresses:
http://spambayes.sourceforge.net
(SpamBayes 1.04)
http://www.comodogroup.com/products/free_products.html
(Comodo AntiSpam)

You can download a FREE personal firewall from the following addresses:
http://www.comodogroup.com/products/free_products.html
(Comodo Firewall)

http://www.ccleaner.com
CCleaner is a freeware system optimization and privacy tool. It removes unused files from your system - allowing Windows to run faster and freeing up valuable hard disk space. It also cleans traces of your online activities such as your Internet history.

http://www.softpedia.com
This is the Softpedia site, a site that has a lot of FREE software.

www.programmingsource.net
This is the link to the site Programming Source Net, there is on the site, among other things, a program that allows you to run multi instances of Yahoo Messenger. Run the program and it is self explanatory. Make sure you use the multi version matching the Yahoo version you are using.

http://mess.be/
It is the link to a site Mess with MSN Messenger it has on the site, among other things, a program that allows you to run multi instances of Windows Live Messenger. Run the program and it is self explanatory. Make sure you use the version matching the MSN Messenger you are using.

http://www.softpedia.com/get/CD-DVD-Tools/CD-DVD-Rip-Other-Tools/DVD-Shrink.shtml
DVD Shrink 3.2 This program allows you to copy DVD's. It allows you to copy dual layer DVD's on a single alyer burner and it removes copywriter and region coding.

http://www.irfanview.com/
It is a link to a free picture editor.

http://www.microsoft.com/windows/windowsmedia/forpros/encoder/default.mspx
This is a link to Microsoft video maker, it is free.

http://www.openoffice.org/
OpenOffice.org is a multiplatform office suite. It is an open sourced project.
Compatible with all other major office suites, Microsoft included, the product is
free to download, use, and distribute.

http://members.freewebs.com/
This is a FREE homepage site. It seems to be quite good.

http://www.zoomshare.com
This is a FREE homepage site, not as good as Freewebs but it has a FREE video/text chat built
in.

I believe that Cam Girls are ripped off by bosses in the industry and cam Girls should work for
them.

I do this purely because I don't like to see people being used and ripped off.

I do NOT work for CTV.

Here, you are an artist or an exotic dancer to bring fantasies to life for others and
to show off just how pretty and sexy you really are.

It's up to you to seduce the members, make them think of you as the hottest
sexist person in the world. Of course, I know you are, and you know you are, but
you have to convince the member.

How do you do it?

Well that's easy. Just brainwash them!

Don't know how to brainwash them? Ok then, it might be a bit harder ;)

Luckily for you, I've compiled a list of some hints and tips that I've seen used by
other models to help you out.

The Basics:

From what I've noticed, the first 30 to 90 seconds are the most important after they've joined the show. They've taken the plunge and willing to shell out at least $1 to see you. This is your chance to make a great first impression. Be interesting and polite and get them engaged with you. Think of yourself as a waitress, welcoming them.

It is better to start a conversation with something like "Hi? I'm YOUR NAME! Thanks for dropping in today to see me, I'm all dolled up here just for you! Hope you're having a good day?" in addition, wave at them.

I see too many people doing the boring "Hi" "how are u?" "Cool. Im' good too." At a bare minimum, the small talk should engage them, not be shy and tiny sentences. If a lot of members are leaving your show right away after joining, consider changing your greeting.

If you can get them to stay a couple minutes, then you've got them.
Now the goal is to keep them hooked so they don't concentrate on the fact that they're spending money, they concentrate on YOU! So engage their attention however you can.

If you have a mic, use it. If you do not have one, get a cheap dollar store one. Sitting and typing isn't as good as talking and most members will leave your show if you're not a really fast typer. Paying money to watch somebody type slow isn't why they joined your show.

Do not be discouraged from a lot of joins and parts by members. They're just window shopping or looking for a quickie. Expect half of the members to do that over the course of an evening.

What to do in a show:

This is something that you should tailor to your own choices, but you should create a routine that you do whenever a new member pops in.

This is especially important when you get a shy member, or somebody who Types slowly (or one handed). They are expecting you to do something for them, even if they don't know what exactly. There should always be motion and action when a member is on camera.

- The more unique or different your shows are, the more likely you will get repeat customers. Themed shows are great!

- Control the pace of the show. Tease them, but don't start anything naughty immediately off the bat

- Use any props and toys that you want.

- Do dress up nights

- Show off various outfits. No rule says you have to wear the same outfit all night after all!

- Role play outfits (schoolgirl, maid, Flight Attendant, etc). Same with Seasonal (Valentine, Easter, Summer, Fall, Halloween, Xmas, etc)

- Have a specific topic/goal for a show

- Do makeup shows or do a tour of your closet.

- Have partners join you on camera for a visit -- Guaranteed to get members to watch you!

- Be Creative! Being unique and interesting is the best thing to do to get members.

- Pace yourself, don't tire yourself out in 10 minutes :)

Promotion:

First thing, you need to make your performer profile steamy and oozing with seduction. That's the first way people are going to get
to know you. If you have a blank/simple/boring profile, expect low interest in your shows. Jazz it up. Put some thought into it and be detailed about what you like doing. One line profiles won't get much of a glance let alone people joining your shows.

You're competing against free webcams on yahoo, you're competing
against all the free porn on the internet (Gals ask yourself this, when was the last time YOU shelled out money for adult materials on the internet?) and yes sadly, even each other.

Link your profile on your yahoo/msn/urnotalone/whatever profile or website. Let everybody in the world know you're available for
Webcam sessions. There's a much better chance that people will join your show if they follow your link.

Change your IM program away message to say you're "camming at ?????? for the evening". That'll help bring people who already love you by for a visit.

If they don't know you're a camgirl, they can't give you money.

Random Thoughts:

- If you're going to do a show from your computer room, PLEASE tidy it up! I saw a show once where I could see dirty dishes and empty chip bags/beer cans in the background.

- If you have a messy/distracting background around you with lots posters or whatever behind you, try putting up a bed sheet or something to get rid of it. The entire focus should be on YOU, not the background. The exception to this is when you are trying to set a mood or create a theme.

- If you are going to drink liquids, use a wine glass even if it is Kool aid :)
- Always be doing something. Lick your lips seductively, move your hands.

Do not be boring.

- Late shows generally produce more quick visits by people who want to play before going to bed.

- A lot of members seem to have a life off the Internet, and Weekend Nights usually have lower numbers then weekdays.

- The longer you're on camera, greater the chance for members. Short shows are useless. This is especially true if it's a random show. If you don't announce it on either your schedule or the Yahoo group, you are at the mercy of the casual surfer. You can be doing other things on, so it can be to your advantage to turn it on and watch a movie or whatever.

- You have to put in time on the camera to meet members and make money.

- Please keep your show times updated. If you cannot make a show and it is in your show times list. Members get very annoyed if your profile says you'll be online at a certain time for a show and you're not.

- Diversify your show times. There are members all over the world, including lots in Europe who are on during the morning.

- If you have a laptop, do a show in your bedroom instead of computer room.

- Always remember you're there for the members, not the other way around.

- The atmosphere and vibe your shows give off is important to repeat business, just like a fancy restaurant.

- Members are visual people. They want to see motion of some sort. Use hand gestures a lot, cross/uncross your legs, laugh, giggle, play with your hair, lick your lips, wiggle your body, anything! Flirt with them. Don't sit there and stare at your monitor and type. I see this so often it's frustrating. Members are not paying to see you sit still; they want to see you doing something, anything. The models that have long shows with members are using their body to get and keep the member's attention.

The more professional you treat it, the more money you will make but that doesn't mean you can't have fun and enjoy yourself at the same time!

For more money, Become a Studio!

http://www.webcammodelstudio.com/faq.html

http://www.izivideochat.com/studio.html

http://studios.cam500.com/

http://www.chatboxxx.com/studio.html

http://www.naked.com/performer/studio.php

http://www.bangstudio.com/webcam/

http://www.skillet.com/webcam/

Camera needed
(Cut and paste the link)
http://www.fumfie.com/pshow/?id=38.6&ref=external

Need to start an at home business without webcam?
Try Solice Moon
http://www.solicemoon.com
sales@solicemoon.com

New Auction Marketplace for new mommies and daddies
Support iKilese.com -http://www.ikilese.com

This website was designed to help moms and dads sell items from home!

This book is to help single moms/dads or people that need extra money. This can be a great income!

Make a free website for your new image!

Here is FREE Hosting websites:
http://myxhost.com/
http://freeadultsitehosting.com/
http://freeadultsitehosting.com/

When you create the website, try to find a niche and fulfill it!

Great Cameras to buy!

List here your webcam websites you can depend on.

_____

_____

_____

_____

_____

_____

_____

_____

_____
_____
_____
_____
_____
_____
_____
_____

List here your most valuable customers:

_____
_____
_____
_____
_____
_____
_____
_____
_____

_____

_____

_____

_____

_____

_____

_____

_____

_____

_____

When you are tired and need the money to flow.
Grab a cocktail! Drink Responsible!

Well so far you have what you need to get going!
The only thing you are missing is starting the
adult business yourself!

Contact my email if you need help!
richcreekfamily@yahoo.com

GOOD LUCK!